Candy for Breakfast

Rebecca Brooke

Name _____

Age _____

Class _____

OXFORD
UNIVERSITY PRESS

OXFORD

UNIVERSITY PRESS

Great Clarendon Street, Oxford OX2 6DP

Oxford University Press is a department of the University of Oxford.
It furthers the University's objective of excellence in research, scholarship,
and education by publishing worldwide in

Oxford New York

Auckland Cape Town Dar es Salaam Hong Kong Karachi
Kuala Lumpur Madrid Melbourne Mexico City Nairobi
New Delhi Shanghai Taipei Toronto

With offices in

Argentina Austria Brazil Chile Czech Republic France Greece
Guatemala Hungary Italy Japan Poland Portugal Singapore
South Korea Switzerland Thailand Turkey Ukraine Vietnam

OXFORD and OXFORD ENGLISH are registered trade marks of
Oxford University Press in the UK and in certain other countries

First published 2005

2023

36

ISBN: 978 0 19 440096 1

Printed in China

Commissioned photography by: Phil James
Illustrations by: Simon Smith (*Illustration page 19 by:* Jackie Snider)

With thanks to Sally Spray for her contribution to this series

Using the book

1 Begin by looking at the first story page (page 2). Look at the picture and ask questions about it. Then read the story text under the picture with your students. **Use section 1 of the CD for this if possible.**

2 Teach and check the understanding of any new vocabulary. Note that some of the words are in the **Picture Dictionary** at the back of the book.

3 Now look at the activities on the right-hand page. Show the example to the students and instruct them to complete the activities. This may be done individually, in pairs, or as a class.

4 Do the same for the remaining pages of the book.

5 Retell the whole story more quickly, reinforcing the new vocabulary. **Sections 2 and 3 of the CD can help with this.**

6 **If possible, listen to the expanded story (section 4 of the CD). The students should follow in their books.**

7 When the book is finished, use the **Picture Dictionary** to check that students understand and remember new vocabulary. **Section 5 of the CD can help with this.**

Using the CD

The CD contains five sections.

1 The story told slowly, with pauses. Use this during the first reading. It may also be used for "Listen and repeat" activities at any point.

2 The story told at normal speed. This should be used once the students have read the book for the first time.

3 The story chanted. Students may want to chant along with the story.

4 The expanded story. The story is told in a longer version. This will help the students understand English when it is spoken faster, as they will now know the story and the vocabulary.

5 Vocabulary. Each word in the **Picture Dictionary** is spoken and then used in a simple sentence.

Wake up May.
It's Monday.
It's a school day.
Come and eat breakfast.

Read and circle.

❶ Where is Mom?

She is in the ⟨bedroom⟩ / kitchen .

❷ What time is it?

It is six o'clock / seven o'clock .

❸ Is it morning or evening?

It is morning / evening .

❹ Where is May?

She is in bed / at school .

❺ Where is May going?

She is going to bed / to school .

Good morning, Mom.
What time is it?

It's seven o'clock.
It's nearly time for school.

Circle yes or no .

1 Monday is a school day.

yes
no

2 May and Mom are in the bathroom.

yes
no

3 It's seven o'clock.

yes
no

4 May is ready for school.

yes
no

5 Can you see any milk?

yes
no

6 May is sleeping.

yes
no

7 Can you see four jars?

yes
no

8 Can you see any bananas?

yes
no

What do you want for breakfast, May?

I'm very hungry. Can I have a candy bar, please?

Find and write.

❶ Carl wants _juice_ for breakfast.

❷ Tessa _____ for breakfast.

❸ Mark _____ for

_____.

❹ I want _____.

You can't have a candy bar
for breakfast, May.
Candy is too sweet.
Do you want an apple?

Write in alphabetical order.

bread

apple

pizza

hamburger

apple

orange

hot dog

banana

cake

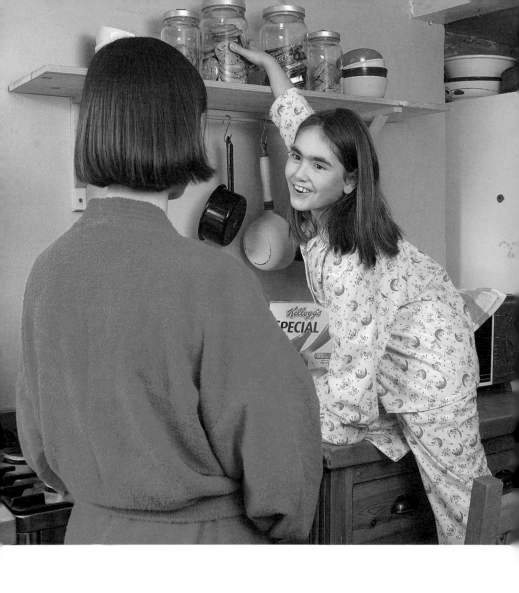

No, Mom, I don't like apples.
Can I have some cookies
for breakfast please?

Rearrange the words.

❶ Monday It is today.

It is Monday today.

❷ likes candy May.

_____

❸ apples She doesn't like.

_____

❹ the is May kitchen in.

_____

❺ wants May cookies some.

_____

❻ too sweet Candy is.

_____

Cookies are too sweet.
They're not good for you.
Do you want a bowl of cereal?

Write Yes, No or I don't know.

❶ May is a girl.

Yes

❷ May likes cookies.

_____

❸ May is six years old.

_____

❹ May is very hungry.

_____

❺ May has school today.

_____

❻ May likes school.

_____

❼ May wakes up at 8 o'clock.

_____

❽ May is taller than her mother.

_____

No, I don't like cereal.
I'm very hungry, Mom.
Can I please have some cake?

Circle each word and write.

1 (May) (is) (a) (student.)

<u>May is a student.</u>

2 Maylikestoeatcookies.

_____

3 Mayisveryhungry.

_____

4 Maydoesnotlikecereal.

_____

5 Maywantssomecake.

_____

6 Mayiscuttingthecake.

_____

7 Mayiswearingpajamas.

_____

Cake is too sweet.
You can't have cake for
breakfast, May.
Do you want some toast?

Complete the crossword.

Matt

Rita

			c						
j	c	o	o	k	i	e	s		

t   m

c   d

a

l

No, Mom, I don't like toast.
Can I have ice cream with
chocolate sauce for breakfast?

1 What do you want for breakfast? Circle four words.

toast cookies milk
cereal apple
chocolate sauce
hamburger ice cream
hot dog
cake
juice
candy bar

2 Write.

I want _____

_____

_____

for breakfast.

Ice cream is not good for
your teeth, May.
Do you want some pancakes?

Number.

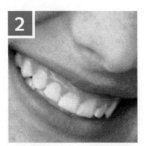

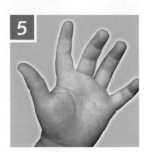

Butter the toast with . . .   3

Bite the apple with . . .

Cook the egg with . . .

Open the cookie jar with . . .

Eat the cereal with . . .

Yes please, Mom. Pancakes with chocolate sauce.

OK, May. You can today, but not every day.

Write the story.

❶ Today is _Monday_ .

❷ It is _____ o'clock.

❸ May wakes _____ .

❹ She has _____ on Monday.

❺ She is very _____ .

❻ She wants to eat a _____ bar.

❼ Her mother says, _____.

❽ May eats a _____ and chocolate sauce for breakfast.

Picture Dictionary

apple

banana

bowl

bread

cake

candy bar

cereal

chocolate sauce

cookie

egg

fork

hamburger

hand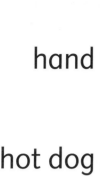

pancake

hot dog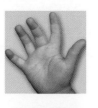

pizza

ice cream

plate

knife

slippers

milk

spoon

orange

teeth

pajamas

toast

Dolphin Readers

Dolphin Readers are available at five levels, from Starter to 4.

The Dolphins series covers four major themes:

Grammar, Living Together, The World Around Us, Science and Nature.

For each theme, there are two titles at every level.

Activity Books are available for all Dolphins.

All Dolphins are available on audio CD.
(2 TITLES ON EACH CD 🔘 SEE TABLE BELOW)

Teacher's Notes are available at **www.oup.com/elt/dolphins**

	Grammar	Living Together	The World Around Us	Science and Nature
Starter	• Silly Squirrel • Monkeying Around	• My Family • A Day with Baby	• Doctor, Doctor • Moving House	• A Game of Shapes • Baby Animals
Level 1	• Meet Molly • Where Is It?	• Little Helpers • Jack the Hero	• On Safari • Lost Kitten	
Level 2	• Double Trouble • Super Sam	• Candy for Breakfast • Lost!	• A Visit to the City • Matt's Mistake	• Numbers, Numbers Everywhere • Circles and Squares
Level 3	• Students in Space • What Did You Do Yesterday?	• New Girl in School • Uncle Jerry's Great Idea	• Just Like Mine • Wonderful Wild Animals	• Things That Fly • Let's Go to the Rainforest
Level 4	• The Tough Task • Yesterday, Today and Tomorrow	• We Won the Cup • Up and Down	• Where People Live • City Girl, Country Boy	• In the Ocean • Go, Gorillas, Go